My Most Beautiful Dream

Mój najpiękniejszy sen

A picture book in two languages

Download audiobook at:

www.sefa-bilingual.com/mp3

Password for free access:

English: **BDEN1423**

Polish: **BDPL2521**

Cornelia Haas · Ulrich Renz

My Most Beautiful Dream

Mój najpiękniejszy sen

Bilingual children's picture book,

with audiobook for download

Translation:

Sefâ Jesse Konuk Agnew (English)

Joanna Barbara Wallmann (Polish)

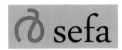

Lulu can't fall asleep. Everyone else is dreaming already – the shark, the elephant, the little mouse, the dragon, the kangaroo, the knight, the monkey, the pilot. And the lion cub. Even the bear has trouble keeping his eyes open …

Hey bear, will you take me along into your dream?

Lulu nie może zasnąć. Wszyscy inni już śnią – rekin, słoń, myszka, smok, kangur, rycerz, małpa, pilot. I lwiątko też. Misiowi także, już prawie oczy się zamykają …

Misiu, zabierzesz mnie do twojego snu?

And with that, Lulu finds herself in bear dreamland. The bear catches fish in Lake Tagayumi. And Lulu wonders, who could be living up there in the trees?

When the dream is over, Lulu wants to go on another adventure. Come along, let's visit the shark! What could he be dreaming?

I już jest Lulu w misiowej krainie snu. Miś łowi ryby w jeziorze Tagayumi. A Lulu dziwi się, kto mieszka tam w górze na drzewach?
Gdy sen się kończy, Lulu chce jeszcze więcej przeżyć. Chodź ze mną, odwiedzimy rekina! O czym on śni?

The shark plays tag with the fish. Finally he's got some friends! Nobody's afraid of his sharp teeth.

When the dream is over, Lulu wants to go on another adventure. Come along, let's visit the elephant! What could he be dreaming?

Rekin bawi się z rybami w berka. Nareszcie ma przyjaciół! Nikt nie boi się jego ostrych zębów.

Gdy sen się kończy, Lulu chce jeszcze więcej przeżyć. Chodź ze mną, odwiedzimy słonia! O czym on śni?

The elephant is as light as a feather and can fly! He's about to land on the celestial meadow.

When the dream is over, Lulu wants to go on another adventure. Come along, let's visit the little mouse! What could she be dreaming?

Słoń jest lekki jak piórko i umie latać! Zaraz wyląduje na niebiańskiej łące.
Gdy sen się kończy, Lulu chce jeszcze więcej przeżyć. Chodź ze mną,
odwiedzimy myszkę! O czym ona śni?

The little mouse watches the fair. She likes the roller coaster best. When the dream is over, Lulu wants to go on another adventure. Come along, let's visit the dragon! What could she be dreaming?

Myszka przypatruje się wesołemu miasteczku. Najbardziej podoba jej się kolejka górska.

Gdy sen się kończy, Lulu chce jeszcze więcej przeżyć. Chodź ze mną, odwiedzimy smoka! O czym on śni?

The dragon is thirsty from spitting fire. She'd like to drink up the whole lemonade lake.

When the dream is over, Lulu wants to go on another adventure. Come along, let's visit the kangaroo! What could she be dreaming?

Smok jest spragniony od ziania ogniem. Najchętniej wypiłby całe jezioro lemoniady.

Gdy sen się kończy, Lulu chce jeszcze więcej przeżyć. Chodź ze mną, odwiedzimy kangura! O czym on śni?

The kangaroo jumps around the candy factory and fills her pouch. Even
more of the blue sweets! And more lollipops! And chocolate!
When the dream is over, Lulu wants to go on another adventure. Come
along, let's visit the knight! What could he be dreaming?

Kangur skacze po fabryce słodyczy i napycha swoją torbę do pełna. Jeszcze więcej tych niebieskich cukierków! I jeszcze więcej lizaków! I czekolady! Gdy sen się kończy, Lulu chce jeszcze więcej przeżyć. Chodź ze mną, odwiedzimy rycerza! O czym on śni?

The knight is having a cake fight with his dream princess. Oops! The whipped cream cake has gone the wrong way!

When the dream is over, Lulu wants to go on another adventure. Come along, let's visit the monkey! What could he be dreaming?

Rycerz i jego księżniczka toczą bitwę na torty. Och! Tort śmietankowy nie trafił do celu!

Gdy sen się kończy, Lulu chce jeszcze więcej przeżyć. Chodź ze mną, odwiedzimy małpę! O czym ona śni?

Snow has finally fallen in Monkeyland. The whole barrel of monkeys is beside itself and getting up to monkey business.

When the dream is over, Lulu wants to go on another adventure. Come along, let's visit the pilot! In which dream could he have landed?

Nareszcie spadł śnieg w krainie małp! Cała zgraja małp jest całkiem poza sobą i urządza przedstawienie.

Gdy sen się kończy, Lulu chce jeszcze więcej przeżyć. Chodź ze mną, odwiedzimy pilota! W jakim śnie on wylądował?

The pilot flies on and on. To the ends of the earth, and even farther, right on up to the stars. No other pilot has ever managed that.

When the dream is over, everybody is very tired and doesn't feel like going on many adventures anymore. But they'd still like to visit the lion cub. What could she be dreaming?

Pilot lata i lata. Aż na koniec świata i jeszcze dalej, aż do gwiazd. To, nie udało się jeszcze żadnemu innemu pilotowi.

Gdy sen się kończy, wszyscy są już bardzo zmęczeni i nie chce im się nic więcej przeżyć. Ale chcą jeszcze odwiedzić lwiątko. O czym ono śni?

The lion cub is homesick and wants to go back to the warm, cozy bed.
And so do the others.

And thus begins ...

Lwiątko tęskni za domem i chce wrócić do ciepłego, przytulnego łóżka.
I inni też.

I wtedy zaczyna się ...

... Lulu's
most beautiful dream.

... najpiękniejszy sen Lulu.

Foto: Ingrid Hagenreich

Cornelia Haas was born near Augsburg, Germany, in 1972. After completing her apprenticeship as a sign and light advertising manufacturer, she studied design at the Münster University of Applied Sciences and graduated with a degree in design. Since 2001 she has been illustrating childrens' and adolescents' books, since 2013 she has been teaching acrylic and digital painting at the Münster University of Applied Sciences.

Cornelia Haas urodziła się w 1972 roku w Augsburgu (Niemcy). Studiowała Design na Politechnice w Münster. Od 2001 roku zajmuje się ilustrowaniem książek dla dzieci i młodzieży. Od 2013 roku wykłada malarstwo akrylowe i cyfrowe na Fachhochschule Münster.

www.cornelia-haas.de

Do you like drawing?

Here are the pictures from the story to color in:

www.sefa-bilingual.com/coloring

Enjoy!

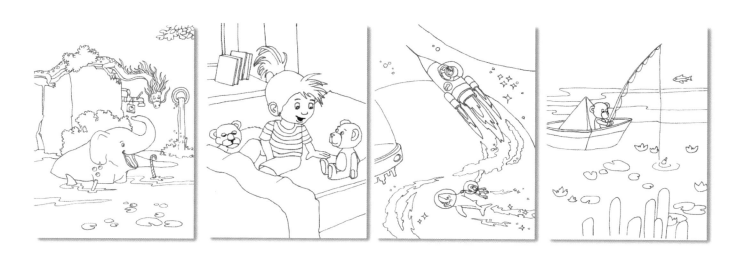

Dear Reader,

Thanks for choosing my book! If you (and most of all, your child) liked it, please spread the word via a Facebook-Like or an email to your friends:

www.sefa-bilingual.com/like

I would also be happy to get a comment or a review. Likes and comments are great TLC for authors, thanks so much!

If there is no audiobook version in your language yet, please be patient! We are working on making all the languages available as audiobooks. You can check the „Language Wizard" for the latest updates:

www.sefa-bilingual.com/languages

Now let me briefly introduce myself: I was born in Stuttgart in 1960, together with my twin brother Herbert (who also became a writer). I studied French literature and a couple of languages in Paris, then medicine in Lübeck. However, my career as a doctor was brief because I soon discovered books: medical books at first, for which I was an editor and a publisher, and later non-fiction and children's books.

I live with my wife Kirsten in Lübeck in the very north of Germany; together we have three (now grown) children, a dog, two cats, and a little publishing house: Sefa Press.

If you want to know more about me, you are welcome to visit my website: **www.ulrichrenz.de**

Best regards,

Ulrich Renz

Lulu also recommends:

Sleep Tight, Little Wolf

For ages 2 and up

with audiobook for download

Tim can't fall asleep. His little wolf is missing! Perhaps he forgot him outside?
Tim heads out all alone into the night – and unexpectedly encounters some friends ...

Available in your languages?

► Check out with our „Language Wizard":

www.sefa-bilingual.com/languages

The Wild Swans

Based on a fairy tale by Hans Christian Andersen

Recommended age: 4-5 and up

with audiobook for download

„The Wild Swans" by Hans Christian Andersen is, with good reason, one of the world's most popular fairy tales. In its timeless form it addresses the issues out of which human dramas are made: fear, bravery, love, betrayal, separation and reunion.

Available in your languages?

▶ Check out with our „Language Wizard":

www.sefa-bilingual.com/languages

More of me ...

Bo & Friends

► Children's detective series in three volumes. Reading age: 9+

► German Edition: „Motte & Co" ► www.motte-und-co.de

► Download the series' first volume, „Bo and the Blackmailers" for free!

www.bo-and-friends.com/free

IT: Paul Bödeker, München, Germany

ISBN: 9783739963464

Version: 20190101

www.sefa-bilingual.com

Printed in Great Britain
by Amazon